AF269329

You Simply Matter

Previously published as "Believe You Matter"

Other Books by Lisa Aré Wulf

You Always Matter
Resting in God's Tender Embrace

Hidden in God's Heart
40 Reflections to Draw You Close to Christ

Reaching for God's Hand
40 Reflections to Deepen Your Faith Journey

Enfolded in God's Arms
40 Reflections to Embrace Your Inner Healing

On a Quest for Christ
Tracing the Footsteps of Your Spiritual Journey

For more information on these titles or to sign up
for Lisa's e-newsletter, please go to LisaAreWulf.com

You Simply Matter

Thriving as God's Beloved Child

by Lisa Aré Wulf

"You're Worth It"
Devotional Series

Spiritual Formation House
Colorado Springs, Colorado

Copyright © 2025 by Lisa Aré Wulf

All rights reserved. No part of this book may be reproduced or transmitted in any form or by any means, electronic or mechanical, including photocopying, recording, or by any information storage or retrieval system without permission in writing from the Publisher.

Scripture quotations are from the ESV®Bible (The Holy Bible, English Standard Version®), copyright© 2001 by Crossway Bibles, a publishing ministry of Good News Publishers. Used by permission. All rights reserved.

Cover Design by Fresh Vision Design
Interior Design by Wood Nymph Creations
Cover Graphic by EnginKorkmaz (Depositphotos.com)
Interior Graphic by Kareemovic_Kareemov1000 (Depositphotos.com)

Library of Congress Control Number 2026901712

ISBN Paperback: 978-1-938042-36-2

Previously published in 2025 under the title "Believe You Matter." This 2026 version is 100% identical to the original content, with updated title references.

Published by Spiritual Formation House
3154 Vickers Drive
Colorado Springs, CO 80918
SpiritualFormationHouse.com

Printed in the United States of America

Contents

Our Journey Begins

Opening Words

Delight yourself in the Lord,
and he will give you the desires of your heart.
Psalm 37:4

What do you want? What do you really want?

For some, the choice is simple. Comfortable lifestyle, awesome friends, or maybe a spacious home.

But for those of us who doubt our worth, the answer is different. We want to be okay. We want to be accepted. We want to matter.

Perhaps these are the secret desires of your heart. If so, you're in luck because Jesus is listening. He's tuned in to your feelings and your pain.

Why not open your spirit to a new reality? Let's walk together through these thirty comforting and inspiring reflections. As we do, you will:

- Learn to see yourself through God's loving eyes.

- Recognize and embrace your true value.

- Find your delight in the Lord who loves you.

Are you ready to thrive as God's beloved child? Yes? Then today's the day to embark on a life-changing adventure. We may discover strengths we never imagined. Through the power of scripture, story, and prayer, we'll heal and move forward. Our souls will be nourished, refreshed, and filled with inner peace.

The spiritual train is in the station, and an epic journey awaits. We might encounter challenges along the way. But with Jesus as our engineer, we can finally uncover the truth—we're worth it.

Time to go. All aboard!

Miss America

Reflection 1

I have loved you with an everlasting love.
Jeremiah 31:3b

Strolling through the state history museum, I spotted an evening gown on display. Large photos in the background told the story of a local girl who became Miss America decades earlier. I heard a noise and glanced around. There she was—the winner herself, now an attractive elderly woman. We had a delightful chat before posing for a quick photo. After a few minutes, I moved on.

I remember that long-ago competition as if it were yesterday. Like a typical kid, I sat curled up in front of the TV. Taking in every detail, I fantasized about being a contestant. I thought Daddy would finally notice me if I became Miss America. Then we'd be happy, and I would be loved.

Sadly, my tale is not uncommon. Many of us question our significance and believe we simply don't count. Whatever the reason, we sense a deep ache inside, a black hole that is never filled. What a heartbreaking way to live.

How about a fresh perspective? From its very first breath, a newborn has value. As the child matures, a unique spark glows ever brighter. Throughout life, this person matters and will always matter. Forever.

Jesus created our baby selves, and we remain the same, just bigger. So, it isn't necessary to achieve greatness or be Miss America. We were worth it then, and we're worth it now. Trust him. He knows.

I have called you by name, you are mine.
Isaiah 43:1c

You Simply Matter

Though I never actually entered a beauty pageant, that didn't stop my obsessive search for ways to be *good enough*. In my younger days, I excelled in music, business, and even politics. You name it, I did it. But the payoff never came. I still felt *less than*. Today I'm ready to accept God's truth. I am as significant and deserving as anyone else.

And so are you. You don't need to perform extraordinary feats to be loved. You don't need to be the best or win a prize. No, you are already special in God's eyes. He's thrilled with who you are.

Ponder and Pray

Have you ever been tempted to prove that you're worthy? What happened?

Does this continue to be a problem? If not, describe your healing.

How do you perceive God's loving presence?

Lord,

You know how I struggle with this. In fact, I've spent ages trying to be at least minimally acceptable. But it's time to pause, turn, and walk in a new direction. Help me understand I am eternally important to you. Amen.

Carrots

Reflection 2

Make me to know your ways, O Lord;
teach me your paths.
Psalm 25:4

"Want a lollipop?" A bank teller held out a bowl filled with sweets. The little girl, who loved running errands with her mom, picked through the selection with glee, skipping all the orange ones. Perhaps she might pick a grape treat or choose strawberry instead. But the orange suckers remained.

The next week was the same as she rejected the orange snacks. She did it the following week too. The teller finally asked why the child kept casting these goodies aside. "Because I don't like carrots."

That young lady could be me. Or you. We all have bothersome situations we'd rather not face. But how often do we mistake a fantastic choice for a problem we are keen to avoid? How many cool experiences do we miss because we can't tell the difference? Quite a few, I'd say!

Why do we do this? Old memories may leave behind a lingering fear. An encounter today could trigger flashbacks to a difficult past. Or maybe we're just dodging anything that reminds us of our earlier pain. This is not good. There must be a better solution.

The world is brimming with countless opportunities waiting to be discovered. And look—Jesus is leading the way, inviting everyone to explore fresh and exciting territory. Let's take him up on it. What do we have to lose? In truth, nothing at all.

Call to me and I will answer you,
and will tell you great and hidden things
that you have not known.
Jeremiah 33:3

You Simply Matter

I have a knack for confusing positive and negative circumstances. I often shy away from trying something new if it reminds me of something else—an unpleasant something else. But appearances can deceive. Two options may seem alike, but that doesn't mean they ARE alike. I need to improve my ability to make sound judgements. Change is hard. But I'm doing my best.

What about you? Perhaps your former worries overlap your current reality. Is this predicament limiting your choices? Don't let it. Jesus stands ready to clear out all your distress. So, what's stopping you? Check out all that he offers today.

Ponder and Pray

When have you mistaken a candy for a carrot, or a similar situation?

Did that limit your life? In what ways?

How could Jesus lend a hand?

Lord,

Fears from long ago continue to hold me back. In fact, this is getting downright tiresome. I know awesome possibilities are around every corner, so help me reach wise decisions. It's time to get moving. Amen.

Rhino Horns

Reflection 3

"We all have a blind spot, and it's shaped exactly like us."—Junot Diaz

Have you seen this cute little meme on social media? A rhinoceros, fancying himself to be a painter, is hard at work in his artist studio. His friend, Mr. Elephant, is posing for a portrait. The painting is lovely except for the enormous horn at the bottom. In fact, every picture on the studio wall features the same rhino horn.

From our viewpoint, it's simple to understand our cartoon friend's blind spot. He faithfully portrayed his view of reality. Yet each canvas suffered from an identical flaw.

Those landscapes and animals didn't have horns. He just thought they did. He painted what he saw.

When distorted perceptions fill our hearts, the rhino in us comes out. For example, we might be so used to shabby treatment that we perceive it everywhere. On the flip side, a kind person's affection for us may go unnoticed for ages.

Let's get real and learn the difference between fact and fiction. Why agonize over issues that don't exist while we deny ourselves the love we deserve? It's time to shift our focus and hand our rhino horns back to Jesus. He's thrilled to restore our 20/20 vision.

Then Jesus laid his hands on
[the blind man's] eyes again;
and he opened his eyes, his sight was restored,
and he saw everything clearly.
Mark 8:25

You Simply Matter

Is my perception skewed? Could be. I have some challenging relationships, but the rest are fine. Yet, I fear I sometimes project imaginary flaws on those who truly wish me well. I've fought this tendency for years and it needs to go. Right now. But how? I'll try this easy recipe—God plus prayer. Then all things will be possible.

Are rhino horns cluttering up your soul? Delete those files right away. Instead, free up space for the images of those who care about you. And don't forget one special item. Jesus would be delighted to send you his very best photo. Just ask him.

Ponder and Pray

Have you ever seen rhino horns that weren't actually there? When?

How could you live a life rooted in truth?

In what ways is God guiding you?

Lord,

Rhino horns appear far too often in my world. I need a heavenly eye exam so I can see clearly. Help me heal and recognize the tenderness that surrounds me each day. Refresh my spirit as we walk together forever. Amen.

The Milk Box

Reflection 4

God saw everything that he had made,
and behold, it was very good.
Genesis 1:31a

My Wyoming home was three blocks from the grade school. In those days, most kids in Cheyenne walked to class. The shortest route passed by a drab little house with a milk box on the porch. Back then, a delivery man carried dairy products house-to-house, leaving them in small, covered containers.

Although I was a talented student as a child, I sometimes made mistakes on my work. Receiving an assignment drenched in red ink left me feeling humiliated. And scared. What would my parents think? Would I be in trouble? Would they ground me—or worse?

I didn't want to find out, so I devised a plan. Passing that house on my way home, I crept up the steps and stuffed the offending paper into the milk box. Then I ran back to the sidewalk and hurried off. Perhaps a kind old lady lived there and was fine with a serving of schoolwork with her cottage cheese. Or maybe not. Who knows?

What a sad story! We long to matter to those we love and to be *worth it*. What a shame when we feel we must hide our blemishes. After all, we're convinced perfection is required to receive affection. Or is it?

Let's ask Jesus. He created us to be humans who mess up. Even children with imperfect homework are awesome in his eyes. So, relax. You are amazing.

For everything created by God is good.
1 Timothy 4:4a

You Simply Matter

All these years later, I'm still the girl who stashed her assignments in a milk box. To this day, I find any less-than-spectacular effort upsetting. Am I really that bad? Of course not. I need to move on. So here's a promise to myself. Next time this situation presents itself, I'll just walk right past that milk box and be myself—warts and all.

What about you? If those feelings of unworthiness don't serve you anymore, why not set them aside? Besides, according to Jesus, they are irrelevant anyway. What does he see when he gazes at you? Only goodness.

Ponder and Pray

Have you ever felt embarrassed by your actions and attempted to conceal them? When?

How else might you handle these situations?

Any thoughts about how Jesus views you?

Lord,

I continue to struggle with issues of worth. Whenever I fall short of my expectations, I become that little girl again. But I know you look at me differently. Help me understand the truth of who I am. Take away my milk box forever. Amen.

Fruit Salad

Reflection 5

Excitement filled the air. Graduation day had finally arrived. In her commencement speech, the top student summed up her college experience in just two sentences. "Knowledge is knowing a tomato is a fruit. Wisdom is not putting tomatoes in a fruit salad."

Funny, but true. It's easy to confuse knowledge with wisdom. Today's world overflows with facts and figures. So much to learn—so little time. Even trying to master a single subject is a heavy lift. And if we're successful, then what? Will happiness and purpose be ours? Maybe yes. Maybe no.

When we don't feel worthy, one solution is to try harder. If we could only get better grades, achieve success in our careers, or retire rich, we'd be fine. After jumping the hurdles and clearing the high bar, we'll matter at last. Or will we?

This problem is pervasive. Like many folks, we suspect we are missing the mark rather badly. We appear confident on the outside, enjoying life and moving ahead. Yet this is often a charade. We wear a false face in public but take it off again at home as we contemplate our shortcomings. We are not okay.

Knowledge benefits us throughout our lives. But to accept our undeniable value, we need wisdom. Let's ask Jesus—the wisest person around. When he says we're worth every ounce of his affection, believe him.

If any of you lacks wisdom, let him ask God,
who gives generously to all without reproach,
and it will be given him.
James 1:5

You Simply Matter

I'll admit it. I haven't always grasped the distinction between knowledge and wisdom. In fact, I've spent years absorbing data—tons of it. But growing older has brought new questions and choices. What about my nagging vibe of unworthiness? Or that unnerving sense of falling short? Today, I'll set them aside and claim the peace and serenity that only wisdom offers.

How about you? Perhaps some sage advice would soothe your spirit. Calm and tranquility can be yours, even in the never-ending quest for knowledge. Simply sit with Jesus and soak up his love. That's all.

Ponder and Pray

How have you seen knowledge and wisdom play out on your journey?

What needs to change? How would you do it?

Where do you see God in this?

Lord,

My mind is overloaded with countless details. I'm overwhelmed and it's all too much to process. A hefty dose of wisdom would be ever so helpful. But where would I find it? I know—with you, of course. Amen.

Horse and Buggy

Commit your way to the Lord;
trust in him, and he will act.
Psalm 37:5

Ever tried to drive a horse and buggy? It's tricky, even on the best of roads. In *Women Talking*, an award-winning film, an older lady struggled to control her two horses, Ruth and Cheryl. The buggy lurched between deep, dangerous gullies. Terrified, she pulled hard on the reins, spooking the horses with her sudden yanking movements.

Then she found a new strategy. Rather than dodging the ruts, she focused her eyes farther up the road. Slowly her hands relaxed and soon each horse was trotting at an easy pace. She had a trouble-free journey and arrived safely.

How about us? Whatever the issue, a mere whiff of distress sends our bodies into panic. Fretting over scary situations doesn't do any good. Our confidence weakens and we fear the worst.

Let's take a lesson from our buggy-driving friend. Instead of staring danger in the face, we can enlarge our perspective and look down the road past the immediate predicament. In short order, we're back on track, with our footing regained, as our buggy glides effortlessly again.

So, what have we learned? A boogeyman might lurk around every corner. Yet the far-off skyline offers hope and serenity. As we navigate bumpy roads, why not loosen our death grip and consider the bigger picture? We're fine. Everything will work out. And see, there's Jesus standing in the distance, beckoning us forward into his arms.

Trust in the Lord with all your heart,
and do not lean on your own understanding.
Proverbs 3:5

You Simply Matter

That buggy story sure sounds familiar. When I stare up close at my difficulties, I'm overwhelmed. But if I gaze outward, all the pieces fall into place. I've decided that the view from 30,000 feet looks a lot smoother. So, I'll give up zigging and zagging. My world is okay. Time to relax.

What about you? Perhaps you have a difficulty that's much too intense. As you step back a bit, those unsettling thoughts recede. And guess what? Jesus is there, offering his hand. So don't dwell on the problem. Just let his peace wash over you.

Ponder and Pray

Are you feeling overcome by something in your life? What is it?

How could you switch your focus to a longer range?

In what ways could God help you cross this terrain?

Lord,

My reality is often frightening. How shall I avoid the perils and pitfalls looming ahead? I'm glad you're there to guide me along the rough spots. Your friendly face is enough. All is well and I am safe. Amen.

Pivot Point

I will instruct you and teach you
in the way you should go;
I will counsel you with my eye upon you.
Psalm 32:8

"Today is the point to which all your yesterdays have been leading since the hour of your birth. It is the point from which all your tomorrows will proceed until the hour of your death."—Frederick Buechner

We each stand in a pivotal place. Our journey has led you and me to this very moment. In fact, our entire family history, stretching back eons, has made us the people we are today. And who knows? Perhaps our ancestors are even peeking over our shoulders, rejoicing in our progress.

Yet a choice looms ahead. We could continue down the same road. If the scenery is delightful and we're enjoying the trip, then why not? Let's stay the course.

But suppose we awoke this morning yearning for something different—a fresh start, a new beginning. Honestly, if our old habits are getting us nowhere, it's best to leave them behind. Change is clearly on the horizon.

But here's the good news. Each day is a pivot point. It's always possible to turn around, refocus, and restart. Maybe a tiny shift is all we can tackle right this minute. That's okay. What we do today sets the stage for our tomorrows—all of them. Each action strengthens our dedication to a brighter future.

And where is Jesus? He's lingering at the crossroads. Our destiny awaits, so why not join him?

> *Your ears shall hear a word behind you,*
> *saying, "This is the way, walk in it,"*
> *when you turn to the right*
> *or when you turn to the left.*
> *Isaiah 30:21*

You Simply Matter

I'm no stranger to pivot points. Over the years, I've had several. Each was a painful trek through a dark and endless wilderness. But I knew if I persevered, a special path would appear. Quickening my pace with every step, I moved ever closer to the dawn. At last, the sun emerged as the landscape cleared, revealing my bold new direction.

Are you at a pivot point? Changing course is a challenge. But remember that all your past experiences have led you here. And Jesus is standing by, eager to take your hand and guide you through.

Ponder and Pray

Have you ever considered a big life change? When?

What brought you there?

Where did Jesus meet you?

Lord,

Facing a pivot point is tough. I know a transition is coming, yet I love my cozy existence. But I'm convinced you'll take me to a lovely destination. So, let's go. Amen.

Inside Out

The Lord sees not as man sees.
Man looks on the outward appearance,
but the Lord looks on the heart.
1 Samuel 16:7b

The elegant tapestry was stunning. Not a stitch was out of place. But this social media post featured a second photo showing the back filled with tangled, unsightly threads. The caption read, "Behind every seemingly perfect person, there's a mess you can't see."

In high school, I learned to be a quick and skillful knitter, turning out sweater after sweater with intricate and colorful designs. They were lovely to behold. But the underside revealed my secret—a haywire jumble of untidy yarn. Not a pretty sight.

Those sweaters reflect the constant battle between our insides and outsides. Friends seem so well put together, while we see only the inner turmoil consuming our hearts. Ironically, these same folks most likely think we're cool and confident. How little they know. Here's the truth. Some people are simply more skilled at masking their chaos.

Yet, the key point is this. Our deepest emotional and spiritual growth happens inside, where the clutter is. And even though our lives feel messy, we are making progress, one muddle at a time. That's something to celebrate.

This inside/outside comparison isn't fair and brings unnecessary heartache. Let's ditch the charade and embrace who we really are, warts and all. After all, Jesus sees everyone from both sides, and he's convinced that you and I are awesome. Why not follow his lead?

He chose us in him
before the foundation of the world,
that we should be holy and
blameless before him.
Ephesians 1:4

You Simply Matter

Okay, I plead guilty as charged. Every day I underestimate myself and overestimate everybody else. But are they fabulous? Am I lower than low? Of course not. I need a dose of reality. I'm not a hopeless wreck, and their polished façade is merely that—a façade. Nobody is as spiffy and smart as they appear. We all stumble and struggle.

You're part of the group, too. Regardless of your experiences, you aren't as flawed as you might think. How am I so sure? Because Jesus has X-ray vision and can peer into your soul. And guess what? He likes what he sees.

Ponder and Pray

Do you ever compare your inner self to someone else's outward appearance?

Is this valid? Why or why not?

How do you suppose Jesus views you?

Lord,

Comparing my inside with other people's outside is a complete waste. But it's so hard to stop. Take my hand and help me understand my value. Let me bask in your love forever. Amen.

Poor Bruno

Reflection 9

For the Son of Man came
to seek and to save the lost.
Luke 19:10

"We don't talk about Bruno!" The young father's voice thundered above the crowd in the school parking lot after the game. A chorus of parents replied, "No, no, no." Their cruelty shocked me—until I discovered they were speaking about a song in a children's movie.

Encanto, an animated motion picture, featured a cast of vibrant characters. But the story excluded a young boy during most of the film. Bruno had told an unwelcome truth to his family, one they refused to hear. Rather than listen, they shunned him instead. Happily, he was welcomed back in the end. Still, his tale is a painful reminder to those facing similar situations.

Families sometimes exclude members who don't fit the mold. As in the movie, groups could be uncomfortable with differing views. Or folks like Bruno may be unfairly blamed or scapegoated to protect others from a reality they choose not to face.

Either way, it is devastating to find ourselves at the center. We're convinced we are at fault. Or worse yet, we suspect we are deeply flawed. But that is simply not the case. This scenario isn't about you or me. No, it's a hurtful drama playing out around us.

If this happens to us, let's keep in mind that we've done nothing wrong. Even in our darkest hour, we are not alone. Jesus is with us. Join him and walk into the light together.

For I will restore health to you,
and your wounds I will heal,
declares the Lord,
because they have called you an outcast.
Jeremiah 30:17a

You Simply Matter

I have so much sympathy for Bruno. Confronting unpleasant truths is difficult because people don't always want to listen. They close the door, and it never reopens. But each voice, including mine, deserves respect and honor. I've found that the best option is to focus on my healing and move forward. Maybe the problem will be resolved. Maybe it won't. But whatever the outcome, my soul is at rest.

And yours can be too. Never forget that you deserve happiness. Jesus understands your pain and loves you no matter what. So, heal your spirit and remember he is your forever friend.

Ponder and Pray

Have you ever felt shunned? What happened?

How did you nurture yourself during this time?

What message was Jesus whispering to you?

Lord,

It's upsetting to be shut out for sharing my thoughts. In fact, it's downright paralyzing. But I know you desire better things for me. Mend my heart and be with me eternally. Amen.

Shine On

I can do all things
through him who strengthens me.
Philippians 4:13

"You don't have to be whole in order to shine." This social media meme says it all.

Think about it. What's the real message in this clever wordplay? It's about the moon, of course. Whatever stage our favorite heavenly body is in, it still shines. A small crescent moon shines. A full round moon shines. Despite being invisible, the new moon continues to shine. We just can't see it.

This meme offers more than a bit of lunar amusement. It provides crucial guidance. As the experts tell us, our competitive world favors only the strongest. To succeed in business or the arts, we must be fabulous. Even to be loved by our families, we must be brilliant. And any whiff of failure sends each of us back to square one. But is that true?

The moon disagrees. It knows that nobody is perfect and we're all a little messed up. Just look at the leading artists and scientists throughout history. Many struggled and were deeply flawed. Yet their successes far outweighed their failures.

Why not join me in accepting the lesson of the meme? We won't let a setback defeat us. And our imperfections will not hinder our progress. Jesus himself understands the moon is right. Even without a telescope, he looks past our mistakes and rejoices in our talents. Let's drop our delusions and believe him instead. We have what it takes.

For I know the plans I have for you,
declares the Lord,
plans for welfare and not for evil,
to give you a future and a hope.
Jeremiah 29:11

You Simply Matter

For years, I relentlessly pursued absolute perfection. The theme song in my childhood home was "when you are good enough, then we will love you." To this day, it's so easy to fall into this hurtful snag. My journey has been long, but I've gradually grown to accept my true self. I'm fine the way I am. And that's the truth.

How about you? If you've bought into this game, it's time to stop. It doesn't matter whether you are a flawless gem or a diamond in the rough. You are valuable, and God is pleased and proud. So, shine on.

Ponder and Pray

Have you felt pressured to be perfect? When?

What could change your mind?

How might Jesus encourage you in this?

Lord,

*Perfectionism is such a snare. It hurts and I need to break
free. But how? My faith is strong, and I trust in your plan.
Please help me relax and shine now and forever. Amen.*

Grandma's Quilt

He heals the brokenhearted
and binds up their wounds.
Psalm 147:3

The Reverend Spencer Brown shared a sweet memory as he launched into his sermon. It seems his grandmother was a quilter. Not simply a quilter, but an amazing artist. In addition to her other creations, she designed a splendid quilt to celebrate his birth.

As baby Spencer grew, he was so fond of his quilt that he chewed on it constantly. A corner finally ripped open. But his grandma rode to the rescue. Sewing a heart-shaped swatch of cloth over the damage, she handed it back to little Spencer with love.

What a delightful tale. Who wouldn't want a caring grandmother to soothe our boo-boos? Or a companion to lend a hand? Or a special someone to cherish and appreciate us? But there are days when our lives go haywire and fall apart. We search everywhere, yet find no friendly offer of support. Suddenly we feel broken, empty, and lost. Will our torn places ever heal?

Yes, they will. But in the meantime, we have choices. Like a grandmother, we could just mend our own wounds. Or advertise for somebody with expert sewing ability. Definite possibilities, but they seem a bit lonely and hollow.

Here's a better option. Why not call on Jesus, our awesome grandparent? His storeroom is chock full of fabric of every color and design. Watch as he selects and stitches the perfect patch. As the psalmist says, he restores our souls.

O Lord my God, I cried to you for help,
and you have healed me.
Psalm 30:2

You Simply Matter

My lovely grandmother was an accomplished seamstress. She's gone now, yet this story reminds me of her. But although she taught me to sew, I much prefer the excellent needlework skills of Jesus. He's always prepared with a mending kit, no matter how tattered the seam or deep the hole. I'm convinced that no injury is too severe for his giant needle and thread.

What about you? Even if you never had a quilt-making grandma, help is near. Whatever your difficulty, whatever your hurt, Jesus is standing by. He'll lift your downcast heart and send you happily out to play.

Ponder and Pray

When has your soul suffered a painful wound?

How did the trouble resolve?

Where did you find Jesus? How did he bind up your spirit?

Lord,

I have too many injuries and too few Band-Aids. My sores just keep festering, and I desperately need your stitching expertise. I know you're not really my grandparent. But with you beside me, my days are as cozy as a baby quilt. Amen.

Labor Is a Pain

Reflection 12

My help comes from the Lord,
who made heaven and earth.
Psalm 121:2

We didn't win. Our childbirth class held a contest after all the babies were born. Each couple submitted a report about their labor and delivery experience. The prize likely went to the most gruesome story. We'll never know.

My husband and I attended every single session, and I memorized all the breathing techniques. In fact, I was certain that if I did everything exactly right, giving birth would be a snap—painless and easy.

Was I ever wrong! It hurt. It really hurt. In those days, natural childbirth was all the rage. Plus, you weren't a real woman if you took pain meds. Thankfully, my labor was quick. But I remember screaming once, and the nurse told me to shut up. She never heard another peep out of me.

Decades later, I found that report in an old storage box. As I read through it, one paragraph stood out—my apology for not performing well enough. Seriously? Not doing labor *well enough*? Most women are simply glad to survive. Yet, I berated myself for not having had a flawless, elegant birth. What an impossible standard!

How often do we beat ourselves up for falling short of an unrealistic target? A lot, but that isn't what Jesus wants. All he asks is that we do our best and leave the rest to him. Let's do just that, celebrating as he carries us over the finish line in his loving arms.

The Lord is my strength and my shield;
in him my heart trusts, and I am helped.
Psalm 28:7a

You Simply Matter

This is so typical. I set that bar way too high and then scolded myself when I couldn't jump it. Even worse, I'm still doing it. Reading this report was an eye-opener. I was clearly wrong to smack myself down over the labor experience. It's time to take a break, examine my life, and make some changes. That's my plan.

Do you do this too? If so, stop. Setting unattainable standards only makes you feel bad about yourself. Aim for realistic goals and give it your all. You'll be thrilled when Jesus hands you a blue ribbon.

Ponder and Pray

When have unreasonable expectations caused you difficulty?

What would have been a better goal?

How could Jesus support you?

Lord,

Why am I so hard on myself? I accomplish a ridiculously difficult feat and then criticize myself because I wasn't perfect. That's crazy, and I'm ready to stop. Help me find a more reasonable reality. You and I can do it. Amen.

The "In" Crowd

I praise you, for I am
fearfully and wonderfully made.
Psalm 139:14

"Belonging is being somewhere where you want to be, and they want you. Fitting in is being somewhere where you want to be, and they don't care one way or the other. Belonging is being accepted for you. Fitting in is being accepted for being like everyone else. If I get to be me, I belong. If I have to be like you, I fit in."—Brené Brown

How true, especially for sensitive souls like us. We yearn to be embraced and understood yet often find that others want us to meet their expectations instead. We're trapped in their mold with no escape in sight.

This isn't easy for kids either. When their families make other plans for them, special talents are quietly set aside.

The result may be decades of sadness, rocky relationships, and strained careers. Sadly, this story is all too common.

But another reality is possible. Even if we've spent ages trying to fit in, the path of self-discovery beckons. We have other choices, and every tiny step toward fulfilling our unique destiny is a win. A new adventure is about to begin. Our chosen life awaits just around the bend.

And what about Jesus? In his eyes, you are one-of-a-kind and truly remarkable. In fact, this old saying tells it all. God didn't create you to be Moses. No, he designed you to be you. And he's delighted with the results.

O Lord, you are our Father;
we are the clay, and you are our potter;
we are all the work of your hand.
Isaiah 64:8

You Simply Matter

My parents had different plans for me. Mother envisioned me as a violinist, and Daddy wanted a party girl. I had a bit of talent, but the hip scene was a total non-starter. It's taken years, but at last I'm becoming who God created me to be. My struggle has been worth it, as I've found so much love and acceptance.

If other folks have unduly influenced you, stop and look around. Jesus is standing right beside you, encouraging your growth, and cheering you on. Watch him provide a loving community as you blossom into your true self.

Ponder and Pray

Do you ever feel you need to be someone else to be liked?

What would it take to reverse course?

How might Jesus help?

Lord,

My road has been long and difficult. But as I'm sure you know, I am slowly letting go of unrealistic pressures. And guess what? It's working out just great. Be with me forever. Amen.

Do Something

Each has his own gift from God,
one of one kind and one of another.
1 Corinthians 7:7b

Five-year-old Landon was obsessed. After seeing a TV show about the USS Arizona, which was bombed at Pearl Harbor in World War II, he set out in his own childlike way to learn all he could. He was thrilled when he got his wish to meet an elderly survivor of the attack.

A short film described their meeting. As little Landon walked confidently with his parents into the room, he handed his new friend a homemade card. Later, they gazed at a flag together as the narrator remarked, "Everyone is big enough to do something." How true. Even this small boy warmed the hearts of many, including the aging sailor.

But perhaps big enough isn't the right phrase. Let's change it to "Everyone can do something." God has uniquely gifted all of us. To one, he gives extraordinary wisdom. To another, he extends the grace of compassion. Some will be famous. Some spend their lives in quiet service. But each person can make a difference.

We might think the young have nothing to offer since they are inexperienced. Likewise, we assume that seniors are of little value once they retire. But everyone has a gift. Everyone has a purpose. Everyone matters.

So don't sit alone, feeling sad or rejected. Cheer up. You're here for a reason, and Jesus is waiting to lead you on an amazing journey. Remember, everyone can do something—even you!

For we are his workmanship,
created in Christ Jesus for good works.
Ephesians 2:10a

You Simply Matter

Okay, there's at least a spark of talent in each of us. But what if I'm the exception? Have I done anything noteworthy? Some days I'm convinced the answer is no. But my family and friends disagree. I matter to them—and to folks I've never met. My challenge is to accept my worth. This is no time to give up.

Do you ever wonder whether your life has an impact? Great question with an easy answer. You may not realize it, but you ARE important. Just ask Jesus. There he is, waving a long list of those you have inspired.

Ponder and Pray

What are your special gifts? Describe them.

How could you best use them?

Where do you see your spiritual path heading?

Lord,

I love the story of little Landon and knowing that everyone has something to contribute. That means me too. But where do I belong? I'm so glad you have a plan for me. Hand in hand, we'll turn it into reality. Amen.

Popeye

*Do not neglect to do good
and to share what you have,
for such sacrifices are pleasing to God.*
Hebrews 13:16

Who remembers this Saturday morning routine? Wake up early. Turn on the TV. Binge on cartoons. Perhaps this custom was before your time. Even so, you may have heard of Popeye the Sailor Man and his giant muscles. Mothers everywhere thank him for getting their kids to eat spinach.

Each episode offered a nugget of wisdom. Devoted fan Kathy Scheiern recalled, "What I took away from watching Popeye was fairly simple. Eat your spinach and be strong. Be who you are and that is enough. Know what matters and stand up for that."

Of course, spinach is a healthy choice even if we don't like it. But Popeye's example reveals much more. His is a story of purpose and value. He calls on us to show the world our true nature and to cherish and protect what we hold dear.

But we're not cartoon characters, and we lead complex lives. A 30-minute solution to our problems would be great, but that's unrealistic. Revealing our authentic selves might be frightening, plus taking a stand often has consequences. We need a dose of Popeye's bravery and strength.

Finally, don't forget the God who sees our warts, picks us up, dusts us off, and loves us anyway. Sometimes our journey feels more like a slog than a delight. But we matter to Jesus. We couldn't ask for a better best friend.

Let us not grow weary of doing good,
for in due season we will reap,
if we do not give up.
Galatians 6:9

You Simply Matter

I adored my childhood animated buddies—Rocky and Bullwinkle, Mighty Mouse, Huckleberry Hound, and...Popeye the Sailor Man. They were a source of endless laughter and fun. Yet each hero confronted the villains. Each hero made courageous choices. These companions gave me the courage to believe in myself. I learned I too can achieve amazing feats. My life mattered.

Did you have a role model when you were young? Or possibly someone you admire as an adult? If so, maybe Jesus put this person, real or fictional, in your path. He thinks you're worthwhile. And he's right.

Ponder and Pray

What experiences inspired you as a child?

How have they affected your life?

Where was God's hand in this?

Lord,

I see your presence at the oddest times, like when you encouraged me through cartoons. Learning to accept my worth has been a lifelong struggle. Yet with your guidance, I'm making progress every day. Soon, my healing will be complete. Thanks, Jesus. Amen.

He's Everywhere

Blessed are the pure in heart,
for they shall see God.
Matthew 5:8

Where is he? I need to find him. Now!

Truthfully, I've been on the lookout for Jesus for years. Sometimes I spot him leaning on his cross at the post office while I stand in line. Or I see him strolling behind me as I push my cart through the grocery store. This began as a lighthearted game when I was a newbie believer. Whatever the scenario, I just wanted him by my side.

Once I attended a large gathering of 5,000 people crammed into a huge convention hall. I scanned the crowd, hoping to catch a glimpse of Jesus. Where could he be? Looking up, I found him at last, swinging on the chandelier. He was having a blast. And I was so glad he was with me.

Okay, let's just say it—this is quirky and totally bizarre. But the point is still valid. Jesus is with us. Maybe we're facing challenges, maybe we feel isolated, or maybe we are celebrating. We never have to search very far. In every situation, he's there.

You may wonder why he would show up for us. Wouldn't he prefer to visit important folks? Powerful leaders? Or beautiful celebrities? No, and here's why. Each of us is embraced by God's love and care. You and I are always worth his time and attention. And look—there he is.

Behold, I am with you always,
to the end of the age.
Matthew 28:20b

You Simply Matter

This is odd, to say the least. Some would even call it downright weird. But I've found this practice helpful in stressful situations. For example, as I await a difficult diagnosis at the clinic, it's so comforting to know Jesus is near. In the silence, his soothing voice calms my anxious soul. I can face any challenge because I'm never alone.

Why not experiment with this little hobby? It might lift your spirit. After all, everyone can use a bit of encouragement, even you. Plus, Jesus is the perfect one to give it—the guy who cares no matter what.

Ponder and Pray

Have you ever imagined that Jesus was nearby? When?

If not, would this appeal to you? How would you try it?

In what ways could this draw you closer to God?

Lord,

I realize it sounds strange, but I believe you are with me. Perhaps it's a hunch. Or a strong sense that you are beside me. Either way, don't stop. Your presence uplifts, sustains, and guides me. I'm certain we'll walk together forever. Amen.

Teresa's Advice

Reflection 17

Draw near to God,
and he will draw near to you.
James 4:8a

"Let nothing disturb you. Let nothing frighten you. All things are passing away. God never changes. Patience obtains all things. Whoever has God lacks nothing. God alone suffices."—Teresa of Avila

A comforting quote, indeed. No matter what troubles we face, no matter what frightening circumstances loom in our path, our spirits remain calm. Why? Because God is with us. He is steadfast and always enough. There's no reason to fret.

Teresa lived in Spain in the 1500s. Life was different back then—and difficult. A reformer, author, and leader, she fought through illness, hostility, and harassment.

According to legend, even her travels were scary. She often entered towns unseen at night to prevent any riots.

In contrast, God was the one thing Teresa never worried about. Her faith was absolute. With him near, she remained sheltered from all harm. Everything would be okay. The God who is unchanging protected her.

It's the same for you and me. Our difficulties may be many, but eventually they will work out. No trouble lasts forever. We need not fear. We need not worry. With God, we are strong. All we need is patience.

As Teresa says, Jesus never changes and if we have him, we lack nothing. In fact, do you see him up ahead, waving in the distance? He meets us at each turn in the road, ready to guide us through any storm.

You keep him in perfect peace
whose mind is stayed on you,
because he trusts in you.
Isaiah 26:3

You Simply Matter

I find personal issues and career challenges to be incredibly stressful. They certainly take their toll. Even the daily news headlines seem unnerving. My mind overflows with anxiety, and I have nowhere to hide. Still, I receive comfort in Teresa's words. Whatever the challenge, it passes sooner or later. Jesus is with me, unchangeable and safe.

Perhaps your world is like this too. But remember—every problem ultimately finds a solution. As medieval Christian writer Julian of Norwich observed, "All shall be well, and all shall be well, and all manner of things shall be well."

Ponder and Pray

Describe a situation that frequently gets you down.

Is a fresh approach possible? What could it be?

Where do you sense God's calming presence?

Lord,

Sometimes I feel terrified, as if I'm trapped with no escape. But is that true? Not really. You're still here. You're still the same. With you, I have all I need. Give me the courage to trust you today and evermore. Amen.

Divine Design

Reflection 18

Do not neglect the gift you have.
1 Timothy 4:14a

The pressure was on. A guest preacher in an unfamiliar church was about to offer a short children's sermon. He invited all the little ones to come forward and bring a prized possession with them. His plan? To improvise and ad-lib about whatever they brought.

A small child gave him an odd-looking toy. Puzzled at first, the pastor realized it belonged to a construction play set. You know, the kind where all the parts interlock.

He lifted the plaything, describing it as an important part of a larger group of pieces. As he launched into a quick Bible lesson, the kids learned that each of them has a special talent. When all these gifts are combined, the result is awesome. The children loved his talk and the treats he handed out afterwards.

And now—an adult point of view. This toy is a vital part of a larger collection. We will understand its true value after the building kit is assembled. Without it, the frame might even collapse.

And why does this matter? Jesus gives spiritual gifts to everyone, including us. Some days we believe it. Some days we don't, especially when our spirits are low. But it's crucial to realize how intertwined all the skills are. Our world would be weaker without us.

Everyone is an essential part of God's plan, so let's use our talents wisely. We sure wouldn't want to disappoint him.

As each has received a gift,
use it to serve one another,
as good stewards of God's varied grace.
1 Peter 4:10

You Simply Matter

Do I really belong? Is there a place for me? Definitely. But I need a fresh perspective to overcome my uncertainty. In the gigantic construction set called humanity, there's room for each of us, regardless of how weird or undeserving we may appear. My contribution to the design is important. If I'm not there, it doesn't hang together. Without me, the project suffers.

Perhaps you feel like a misplaced building block and wonder if anyone cares. Time for a reality check. You matter to tons of people. And who would miss you the most? Jesus, of course. Don't let him down—join the team.

Ponder and Pray

Describe a quality you have that could benefit others.

How could you apply that attribute?

How does your faith factor in?

Lord,

Sometimes I struggle to discover my purpose. Where do I fit in? What can I contribute? It's a mystery to me, but you have the answer. Guide me with your gentle hand along my unique path. Amen.

It Never Happened

Let not your hearts be troubled.
Believe in God; believe also in me.
John 14:1

"I remember the story of the old man who said on his deathbed that he had had a lot of trouble in his life, most of which had never happened."—Winston Churchill

Ouch! I recognize myself. Do you?

We're weighed down with so many worries. We can't begin to count them all. One of my talents is an uncanny knack for sensing impending doom. After scanning the horizon for threats, my brain moves at lightning speed through every conceivable scenario. Then I meticulously select only the best and safest strategies to keep out of harm's way.

But here's the catch—none of these situations are real. Most likely, 99% of them will never materialize. What a ton of mental gymnastics for stuff that just won't happen. But I do it anyway. Somehow this protects me.

Or does it? When we focus all our attention on possible perils, we overlook the positive in our lives. We might be worried about our jobs and overlook our child's happy smile. Or a loved one's frown could signal relationship issues when this person merely has a headache. Talk about overreacting.

Yes, we all have potential problems. And few, if any, will actually occur. So, rather than worrying, how about fixing our eyes on Jesus? Now that's a more productive plan. In fact, there he is, guiding us along. He'll take care of everything.

And the peace of God,
which surpasses all understanding,
will guard your hearts and your minds
in Christ Jesus.
Philippians 4:7

You Simply Matter

Danger detection is my specialty, and I am a pro at finding it anywhere. My mind instantly kicks in as I brainstorm 50 solutions before anyone even suspects a problem. This is how I stay safe. But at what cost? Being terrified of imaginary bogeymen is nobody's idea of fun. Time to put God back on my radar screen.

Perhaps you struggle with this too. But you don't need to. Why fret over difficulties that may never come to pass? Turn your true burdens over to Jesus, instead. He's the guy with the answers. Trust him.

Ponder and Pray

Do you stress over unlikely events? When?

What else could you be doing?

How would it feel to trust God in these circumstances?

Lord,

I'm a champ at conjuring up hazards and can chart multiple paths to safety in the blink of an eye. But how does this help? It doesn't. Trusting you is a much better policy. Please hold my hand and protect me forever. Amen.

Send Them Back

Reflection 20

For you formed my inward parts;
you knitted me together
in my mother's womb.
Psalm 139:13

My mother was quite the activist—in an odd sort of way. During my childhood, the topic of zero population growth was all the rage in the United States. This strategy addressed the emerging global overpopulation crisis. But she took it a step further. She called her new concept retroactive birth control, or "if you don't like your kids, send them back."

Of course, this proposal was a fantasy and completely unworkable. Even so, she offered her grand solution with unrestrained glee to anyone who would listen. Her short, catchy sales pitch was especially amusing when her own young family was present. Amusing, that is, to my mother and her friends. They loved the idea. But I felt only shame and humiliation. Would she actually send us back?

This scheme was nuts! It only valued children if they were likable enough. That could include being attractive, accomplished, athletic, or any other trait the parent desired. If the little ones didn't measure up, they were gone, no questions asked.

What do you suppose God thinks about retroactive birth control? My guess is not much. He recognizes the unique qualities of each person despite their flaws and imperfections.

We each possess an intrinsic worth that can never be taken away. Everyone matters. So, the next time difficulties get us down, let's check out God's perspective. He knows we are lovely beyond words.

Before I formed you in the womb I knew you,
and before you were born I consecrated you.
Jeremiah 1:5a

You Simply Matter

I lived in constant fear of being sent back. Staying upbeat was tough knowing my world could crash at any moment. Plus, it was downright loony and totally weird. But I've healed and moved on. We all have a purpose, and we all are welcome—even me. It's comforting to know Jesus is standing by, his arm around my shoulder, keeping me safe.

You are also protected because you belong to Jesus. The earth won't open and swallow you up if you aren't perfect. So, stop worrying and be at peace. You are resting in the shelter of God's grace.

Ponder and Pray

Do you ever fret about really bizarre stuff? When?

What's a reasonable plan to set these worries aside?

How might Jesus support you in this?

Lord,

I know this situation was bonkers, yet it affected my soul, my confidence, and my sense of safety. But I am convinced that you have wonderful plans for me. Stay with me as we do life together. Amen.

*H*ope

Reflection 21

And now, O Lord, for what do I wait?
My hope is in you.
Psalm 39:7

"Despair is where hope is born."—Jonathan Trotter

Her world was dreary, with troubles piled so high she couldn't see past them. Since losing her husband, one thing after another had gone wrong.

Her boss at work was demanding. Reliable childcare was expensive when she could find it at all. Even her car was acting up. And this didn't include the ongoing battle to pay rent, buy groceries, and handle the bills. She felt overwhelmed, and despair was her constant companion.

Our own circumstances may not be as dire, but tough times still chip away at our confidence. When we reach a breaking point, a miracle seems like our only way out. Any miracle will do. As we wait, our hearts cry out, "Please, God, help me now!" Maybe he will. Maybe he won't. Jesus is an amazing friend, but he doesn't grant our wishes every time.

Perhaps our definition of hope needs a makeover. Noted playwright and European leader Vaclav Havel wrote, "Hope...is not the conviction that something will turn out well, but the certainty that something makes sense, regardless of how it turns out."

This new insight offers a fresh perspective on God's wisdom. We know we won't get everything we want. But can we count on Jesus no matter what? You bet. He's always looking out for us. So, let's ditch the despair today and give God a chance.

I wait for the Lord, my soul waits,
and in his word I hope.
Psalm 130:5

You Simply Matter

Life isn't easy, especially when I feel lost and unsure. What will I do? Is everything going to be okay? Then a flicker of light appears without warning. An uplifting hymn in church. A surprise call from a special someone. Or a kind gesture from a stranger. Although my pesky problems remain, my gloom lifts. Perhaps this is how Jesus answers my prayers.

Is it the same for you? It's possible you've prayed about a stubborn situation with no apparent response. Yet God is not ignoring you. His actions might seem puzzling. But eventually all will be well.

Ponder and Pray

When have you faced a major obstacle?

What did you pray for? How did God answer?

Were you able to accept his reply?

Lord,

My reality is sometimes dark and full of struggle. I long for your aid but can't tell if you're listening. Then suddenly you arrive, ready to save the day. You are my hero. Don't stop—I need your help every hour. Stay with me forever. Amen.

Spit It Out

I have fought the good fight,
I have finished the race,
I have kept the faith.
2 Timothy 4:7

William Wilberforce was a man on a mission. As a member of Parliament in the early 1800s, he committed his life to stopping the slave trade in Great Britain. The film, *Amazing Grace*, recounts his long and arduous fight.

The battle was overwhelming, and he was exhausted. As the years dragged on, he considered abandoning his crusade. He still believed that slavery was evil. But bowing out and watching from afar was definitely attractive.

When his wife gave him this advice, he reconsidered. "If you have a bad taste in your mouth, you spit it out. You don't continually swallow it back."

How many times do we stifle our voices, choosing to hide our opinions instead? Perhaps our spirits yearn to express passionately held truths. Or maybe we encounter hurtful remarks and hope to offer a healing perspective. Yet fear stands in the way. Despite the bitter aftertaste, words remain unsaid.

But here's the truth—our viewpoints matter. We deserve to be heard. As we walk life's path, challenges must be tackled and injustices healed. We can't stay quiet forever. And we don't have to.

It takes guts to stand up for ourselves. But our well-being is at stake. So, let's spit it out and move ahead. And guess what? Jesus is standing by with a cup of tasty mouthwash, just for us.

He who began a good work in you
will bring it to completion.
Philippians 1:6b

You Simply Matter

Speaking up is a challenge. Whether it's a minor issue or a huge concern, I have a problem. Unless the situation is totally safe, I rarely open my mouth. But I don't want a bad taste for the rest of my days, either. It's time to grab my courage with both hands, be bold, and face my fears.

You may be in the same boat. Why spend your life wishing you were brave enough to speak? Remember, Jesus is right there with you. He's your greatest cheerleader. So...spit it out. You'll be glad you did.

Ponder and Pray

Is something weighing on your heart?

If you merely swallow it back, how would you feel?

In what ways could Jesus help?

Lord,

You know I am passionate about certain topics. Some are matters of great importance. Some are tiny pet peeves. In any case, I struggle to share my feelings. But when I'm silent, my world is sad and empty. Please fortify me with your strength as I say what needs to be said. Amen.

Hate Nothing

Give thanks to the God of heaven,
for his steadfast love endures forever.
Psalm 136:26

Jesus found me later in life. As a new follower, I had lots to learn. I paid close attention every Sunday and at the Wednesday night classes too. Yet fear nagged my soul in those early days. Did God regret creating me? Was he sorry I was alive?

One day my doubts vanished. A few weeks before Easter, I attended a special service. A reading from the Book of Common Prayer offered these reassuring words: "Almighty and everlasting God, you hate nothing you have made." Whenever this season rolls around, I long to hear this promise again. God is glad that I'm here. He knows my value. I matter to him.

Many of us struggle to appreciate our worth. Perhaps others have said we are undesirable, or we see ourselves as *less than*. Maybe we're convinced God could never care about us. Worse still, what if he genuinely dislikes us?

None of this is true. Let's believe instead what the prayer says—God hates nothing he has made. That means nothing. Not you. Not me. Not hate. Only love.

How soothing. No matter what we've done or the mess in our lives, Jesus offers his supportive presence. Mistakes may litter our paths, but forgiveness is always available.

Next time you're wondering how Jesus feels about you, remember this prayer. He's in your corner and with you all the way. Never forget it.

As the Father has loved me,
so have I loved you. Abide in my love.
John 15:9

You Simply Matter

I know it sounds odd, but this truly upset me. I struggled to believe that God cared about me, despite all my flaws. I even questioned my Christian friends about the Bible. Did God really look upon his whole creation and declare it to be good? They said he did, and that I had nothing to fear. Everything was fine, and I was okay.

Why not let this comforting message soothe your heart, too? Whatever fumbles or wrong turns you take, Jesus stands ready to encourage you. In fact, he's right there, waiting to enfold you in a big hug.

Ponder and Pray

Have you ever worried that Jesus thinks badly of you? If so, when?

How were you able to reassure yourself and settle this question?

What sign did he give to show you he cares?

Lord,

It's taken me a long while to leave behind these feelings of unworthiness. Negative thoughts do pop up now and then. But I rarely doubt your affection. I will dwell in your house forever. Amen.

Flying Golf Clubs

Repay no one evil for evil,
but give thought to do what is
honorable in the sight of all.
Romans 12:17

"Always throw your golf club in the direction that you're going. Don't get mad. Don't get even. Just get ahead." Former President Ronald Reagan's words offer a fresh approach to tackling tough situations.

Let's put it another way. Why waste your energy on rage and resentment? As Pamela Short writes, "The best revenge is none. Heal, move on, and don't become like those who hurt you."

We've all seen this movie before. Someone wounded us. Someone did something awful to us. Someone wrecked our lives. We're devastated and obsessed. We long to harm them as much as they harmed us. Or even more. These people must be held accountable—right away!

But this is a bad idea. Does constant fighting do any good? Would more conflict mend our souls and cheer our spirits? No, it merely traps us in a never-ending downward spiral. How will we escape?

Now's the time to update our tactics. For example, a gracious reply instead of anger could shift the dynamics. A small positive change starts us on the path of healing and peace. As our new life journey unfolds, we will be happy and free.

Facing a rough situation? Why not simply chuck your golf club across the green? Now, that's a better choice. Plus, Jesus is standing in the distance, ready to catch it.

See that no one repays anyone evil for evil,
but always seek to do good
to one another and to everyone.
1 Thessalonians 5:15

You Simply Matter

When I'm frustrated, it's just so hard to toss my golf club. Beating my adversary over the head with it feels much more rewarding. But does that truly fix anything? Does it bring happiness and satisfaction? Not really. I'm learning to stop, think first, and avoid disaster. A more reasonable reaction is elegant and effective. It gets me where I want to go.

What about your golf club? If you're using it to make your enemy miserable, why not let Jesus gently fling it forward for you? Then you can walk together to retrieve it and continue the game.

Ponder and Pray

When problems arise, do you seek to get even? Describe.

How might you consider a different response?

In what ways could God help you?

Lord,

I sometimes get so angry that retaliation seems to be my best option—indeed, my only option. But it's useless and fixes nothing. Please show me a more fruitful strategy so we'll be totally awesome golf buddies. Amen.

Mrs. Harris

Reflection 25

For the needy shall not always
be forgotten, and the hope of the poor
shall not perish forever.
Psalm 9:18

She was a nobody. As a lowly cleaning lady, she barely earned enough money to live on, all the while enduring daily criticism and insults. Night after night she trudged home to a skimpy dinner in her run-down London apartment. A middle-aged widow, she lived alone. Ignored and forgotten, her soul was invisible.

One day a dream captured her heart—an unrealistic dream. She saw a designer evening gown and was determined to travel to France and buy it. Never mind that she had no place to wear such a dress. Yet her bleak existence improved. Planning her trip consumed every minute as she patiently saved her pennies.

The sweet film, *Mrs. Harris Goes to Paris*, told the story of an unimportant lower-class woman. Predictably, the fashion elite scorned and shunned her. But common folks rallied to her side. In a dramatic turn, this ordinary person ignited hope for scores of people just like her. Even a nobody can make a difference.

What about us? Our planet is too crowded, too busy, and too noisy. Who would notice us? What could we possibly contribute? Will we ever truly matter?

In short, yes, and we already do. Mrs. Harris made her mark by stepping out with courage and by being herself. We can too. It's time to unveil our real selves. When we do, lives will change, including our own.

Blessed are you who are poor,
for yours is the kingdom of God.
Luke 6:20b

You Simply Matter

Some days my life seems so dull and monotonous. Do I accomplish anything meaningful? Am I making an impact at all? Though I have my doubts, Jesus has the answer. I may minimize my efforts, but he knows I have encouraged others through my example. I might seem insignificant, but reality paints a different picture. No one is invisible.

It's the same for you. Perhaps this is a moment for serious self-reflection. You are valuable to yourself and important to so many close to you. And look, there's Jesus up ahead, holding a blue ribbon just for you.

Ponder and Pray

Have you ever felt unseen? When?

What if you could open your eyes and see your actual influence? How would that affect you?

Where is God in your struggle?

Lord,

There are moments when I am convinced I'm a real loser with nothing to offer. But you know that's not true. Help me remember all those I've inspired and helped. And please don't stop sending them to me. Amen.

Tidying Up

For where your treasure is,
there your heart will be also.
Matthew 6:21

"The first step in crafting the life you want is to get rid of everything you don't."—Joshua Becker

Tidying up is all the rage these days. Famous authors and experts offer advice on what to keep and what to toss. As we pare down to the bare essentials, our souls will find rest, as peace and tranquility surround us. Or so they say.

But this is easier said than done. As we age, things pile up. That's just how it is. Some are valuable. Some hold tender memories. Some are only junk. Tidying up can be hard—ridiculously hard.

How about our personal lives? In our hearts, we imagine an ideal world. Dreams always come true. Love, success, and anything we desire can be ours. Yet these wishes remain stubbornly outside our grasp. Why? Something is separating us from our hopes for the future.

Let's circle back to the beginning. What fits into our perfect life? What's worth keeping and what should we scrap? Streamlining our physical space isn't the only issue. Old emotional baggage holds us down too. But letting go opens opportunities for fresh choices. Are we on the right path? Would another direction be better?

Such decisions require prayer, reflection, and soul-searching. Where are we called? What delights our spirits? These questions are between each person and God. So why not ask? He's always thrilled to hear from us.

For what does it profit a man
if he gains the whole world
and loses or forfeits himself?
Luke 9:25

You Simply Matter

I've hit my limit, and it's time to de-clutter. I mean seriously de-clutter. I have generations of stuff in my home. Some items are sweet reminders of the past. Others only litter up the house. But overcoming inner challenges is the hardest. Each year I set a goal to heal one dysfunctional mindset. Progress is slow, but someday I hope to be tidy at last.

How's your decluttering going? It can be tough to part with treasured possessions. And mending earlier wounds is even harder. But you can do it. With a tiny effort every day, amazing results will soon emerge. Jesus would be so proud.

Ponder and Pray

Do your belongings or habits prevent you from moving forward?

How might you release them?

What support could Jesus provide?

Lord,

I know a deep clean is long overdue. That means physical, emotional, and spiritual cleansing. What a challenge, especially for someone like me. But I believe I'm up to the job. Help me focus on what truly matters. Amen.

The Soda Machine

Reflection 27

God is love, and whoever
abides in love abides in God,
and God abides in him.
1 John 4:16b

Excitement filled the air as my graduation day dawned. Political unrest and war had marred my high school years. Yet today was a time to celebrate new beginnings and bright futures.

Decked out in my white cap and gown, I took my seat with the class. As I prepared to walk onstage, I quickly glanced into the audience. My mother was nowhere to be seen. She had apparently stepped out into the hallway for a break.

The soda machine outside the auditorium was in great demand on this hot June afternoon. Unlike other vending machines, this vintage model poured liquid into paper containers. But alas, it had run out of cups. Folks inserted coin after coin only to sadly watch their drinks disappear down the drain. My mom thought this was hysterically funny and a welcome change from the stuffy ceremony. She missed my big moment.

Being ignored by those we care about is heartbreaking. Their thoughtless actions are often deeply painful. But remember, this rudeness says more about them than about us. We are worthy of respect. Our lives are valuable, and nothing can diminish our spirits. Nothing.

And what does Jesus think about this? In short, he has our backs and is excited to support us anytime and anywhere. In fact, there he is, whistling and clapping as he cheers us on.

He will rejoice over you with gladness;
he will quiet you by his love;
he will exult over you with loud singing.
Zephaniah 3:17b

You Simply Matter

It's tough when others reject us. Their behavior speaks loudly as our hearts sink in despair. I've felt that way too, questioning why this happened to me. What have I done to deserve it? If I try to figure it out and can't, the issue is likely about them. Still, convincing myself is never easy.

Do you struggle with this too? Does your self-esteem take a hit when you're rejected, overlooked, or forgotten? I'll bet it does. But keep in mind that you have a friend who won't ever forsake you. Jesus is always there, eager to lift your soul.

Ponder and Pray

Describe an occasion when a loved one seemed to disrespect you.

Ponder the situation. What led to the problem?

How might God help you heal from situations like this?

Lord,

Rejection stings, especially from those who are close to me. I just don't know how to cope, and I need your soothing touch. Please stitch up these wounds and mend my broken heart. Amen.

Catch That Tune

Blessed are the meek,
for they shall inherit the earth.
Matthew 5:5

The pastor was obsessed with last night's symphony concert. He couldn't resist sharing one highlight in his sermon. At a climactic moment, the piccolo, a tiny high-pitched flute, had made quite a dramatic entrance. "Without that piccolo," he explained, "the finale would have been a dud."

That's possible. But was he being fair? We all know that piccolos are cool. But what about the less glamorous instruments? Aren't they also essential members of the orchestra?

Consider the viola. It looks like a violin, but a tad larger. Viola music can be pretty dull. This could explain why these players are often eclipsed in concerts. In fact, if crash dummies replaced the whole viola section, would anyone notice? Maybe not. How sad.

But let's double back to that minister and his sermon. Perhaps he really meant to say that all performers matter and all are critical. Any absence leaves a void. The viola section is a perfect illustration. Its sound may be subtle, yet every musician is vital for a successful performance.

Just like these instruments, each person is irreplaceable in life's ensemble. That includes us. Some days, we doubt our contribution to the world. Are we enhancing the melody of life? Does our presence make a difference? Well, Jesus knows it does. Regardless of how small our part or faint our voice, we count. All songs are special to God—even ours.

Take my yoke upon you, and learn from me,
for I am gentle and lowly in heart,
and you will find rest for your souls.
Matthew 11:29

You Simply Matter

Okay, I'm definitely biased since I was a viola player. Was I important to the orchestra? Sure. Did I believe it? Not always. But while our group seemed invisible at times, the viola players had loads of fun. Rather than engage in rivalry, we went out to lunch instead. What a win-win combination—beautiful music and good friends.

Do you wonder whether anybody sees your efforts? Why not ask Jesus? He'll answer with a resounding YES. His creation would be dreary indeed if you weren't here. So, hang in there. You're no crash dummy!

Ponder and Pray

Have you ever felt unseen? When?

Was there a silver lining in your situation?

How did Jesus help you claim your worth?

Lord,

When famous people are missing, everyone notices. But what about me? Am I just background noise in the greater universe? Of course not. Show me my role in the harmony of your masterpiece. It's you and me—musicians forever. Amen.

Ripen, Ripen, Ripen

Be still before the Lord
and wait patiently for him.
Psalm 37:7a

"How does an apple ripen? It just sits in the sun. A small green apple cannot ripen in one night by tightening all its muscles, squinting its eyes and tightening its jaw in order to find itself the next morning miraculously large, red, ripe, and juicy beside its small green counterparts."—James Finley

That poor little apple was trying too hard. It probably spent all evening chanting, "Ripen, ripen, ripen." But at dawn, it appeared no redder than before. How disappointing!

Some things just take time. If we go to bed with a broken arm, we won't be doing push-ups in the morning. Healing is a process, and patience might be our only option.

Are we more like that tiny apple than we care to admit? When faced with a difficult situation, who among us hasn't desperately sought a quick and easy answer? Nobody wants to sit around forever, wishing and hoping for a solution. Yet we may not have much choice, especially if the remedy lies outside our power. Maybe there's nothing we can do, so we wait.

Patience is essential to our emotional and spiritual well-being, too. Discovering our true selves is an unfolding journey. Thankfully, Jesus is on board and always with us. As James Finley says, "We must wait for God, we must be awake; we must trust in his hidden action within us."

The Lord is good to those who wait for him,
to the soul who seeks him.
Lamentations 3:25

You Simply Matter

My skill set has never included slowing down. I'm a fast-track, results-oriented person. Why bother with ten steps if four will get the job done? But inner growth doesn't happen overnight. It could be months or even years until I notice any difference. Still, I am learning how to press pause. Transformation happens, and my progress is real.

And you? The road to wholeness and peace is full of detours. It's no fun to be blocked by delays. But Jesus is standing by, ready to help. Follow his lead and move ahead, one step at a time.

Ponder and Pray

Are you struggling with a never-ending issue? What is it?

How could you relax a bit and be patient?

Where do you see Jesus in this?

Lord,

You know me. When I face a challenge, I'll run a hundred miles an hour to fix it. But is this really a good strategy? Perhaps it's better to catch my breath, accept reality, and open myself to your path. Take my hand while you show me the way. Amen.

Those "R" Words

Reflection 30

Behold, I am doing a new thing;
now it springs forth,
do you not perceive it?
Isaiah 43:19a

This was it. Story over. Time to sign off and move on, at least from her current career. Arriving at the office on her last day, she received a lovely send-off. But when asked to share a few thoughts, she echoed the animated TV series character Megabyte. "This is not the end. I have zero intention of fading away. So today I am putting the 'R' words into action. And this is my favorite—REBOOT!"

Retirement is an "R" word. It sounds attractive, but the initial charm quickly wears off for some. We feel discarded and cast off, like an old cow put out to pasture. But folks like us are in luck. Who says retirement must be a single event? We can re-imagine ourselves as often as we want.

Don't lose heart when one road ends. A brand-new direction awaits exploration. We could renew, rekindle, or reclaim a forgotten interest. Or enjoy a season of refreshing, restoring, or recharging. Maybe even reawaken, recreate, or resurrect a talent we set aside long ago. So many "R" words—so little time.

Our journey is not over merely because we've reached a certain age. There are places to discover, skills to master, and friends to find. Let's revitalize, renovate, and—when we're tired—rest.

The "R" words keep our feet on the path and our eyes on God. In fact, if we look closely, we'll catch him winking in delight.

I will give you a new heart,
and a new spirit I will put within you.
Ezekiel 36:26a

You Simply Matter

I've never been one to just call it a day. Each year, when my birthday comes and goes, I wonder what I'll leave behind. Did I make an impact? Am I building a legacy? Who knows? But I'm not done yet. Full steam ahead!

What's your perspective on all those "R" words? Perhaps they haven't appeared on your radar screen so far. But there's hope. No matter your years, Jesus isn't through with you. He has tons of projects and cool happenings available. Take your pick. You'll be glad you did.

Ponder and Pray

Picture your future. What do you see?

Are you open to a change of plans?

How could Jesus help you figure out your next step?

Lord,

I am clueless about what might be in store for me. Some days I only want to unwind and chill. Other times, I'm eager to scout out whatever is around the corner. Show me the way. Amen.

Our Journey Continues

Closing Words

The Lord will keep your going out
and your coming in
from this time forth and forevermore.
Psalm 121:8

My friend, our adventure together is nearing an end. And what a trek it has been. We have shared stories and reflections about our lives. Scripture and prayer have touched our hearts. Along the way, our spirits grew strong as our true worth went on display for everyone to see.

It's time to rest a bit in the cool afternoon shade. During this pause, why not celebrate all you've discovered as you ponder your next steps? Remember, you are never alone. The one who delights in you stands right by your side.

And now may you go forth and flourish as God's beloved child. As you walk his sacred path, keep in mind that Jesus is looking out for you. Each day he protects you as you venture out and nourishes you upon your return. His love never ends.

As we part, I offer these final words of encouragement:

> Let us experience joy.
> Let us live in hope.
> Let us know God's love.

May the grace of God be with you now and always. Amen.

Request and Invitation

Hi friend,

Thanks so much for reading *You Simply Matter*. Hope you found it uplifting and encouraging.

Would you consider writing a quick review, even a sentence or two? Reviews are ever so helpful to authors like me. I invite you to post one with your favorite online bookseller today. It's super easy and only takes a couple of minutes.

I'm also delighted to invite you to subscribe to my e-newsletter. Why not enjoy a sprinkle of inspiration to brighten your day. My husband and I offer this through our ministry, Spiritual Formation House.

Interested? Hop on over to LisaAreWulf.com and click the subscribe button. I'll take it from there.

Thanks again—sure appreciate you!

Lisa

About the Author

Lisa Aré Wulf is an award-winning women's devotional author. Her print, audio, and e-books have been finalists in the USA Best Book Awards, the Independent Author Network Book of the Year Awards, the Next Generation Indie Book Awards, and the Voice Arts Awards.

Publications across the country have featured Lisa's articles on Christian living and spiritual growth. As a speaker, she shares her faith with transparency and grace.

A graduate of Fuller Theological Seminary, Lisa also holds two degrees from the University of Colorado. She is an adjunct accounting professor, owned a CPA firm, served in elected public office, and was a professional orchestral musician.

Lisa and her husband, Calvin, enjoy the mountain scenery at their Colorado home. For more information about Lisa Aré Wulf or to sign up for her e-newsletter, please visit LisaAreWulf.com.

www.ingramcontent.com/pod-product-compliance
Lightning Source LLC
Chambersburg PA
CBHW021657070726
47591CB00017B/641